J. Calvin. Bushey

Sparkling gems nos. 1

J. Calvin. Bushey
Sparkling gems nos. 1
ISBN/EAN: 9783337806668

Printed in Europe, USA, Canada, Australia, Japan

Cover: Foto ©ninafisch / pixelio.de

More available books at **www.hansebooks.com**

SPARKLING GEMS

Nos. 1 & 2
✵COMBINED.✵

A NEW AND CHOICE COLLECTION OF MUSIC FOR

SABBATH SCHOOLS, TEMPERANCE,

—AND—

SOCIAL MEETINGS.

✵BY J. CALVIN BUSHEY.✵

PUBLISHED BY
WILL L. THOMPSON & CO.,
EAST LIVERPOOL, OHIO.

Price, Board Covers, 20 cts. each; $2 per dozen by mail or express, prepaid; or $1.80 per dozen by express, not prepaid.

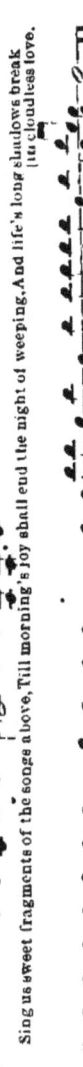

BRIGHTER WHEN NEARER TO THEE.

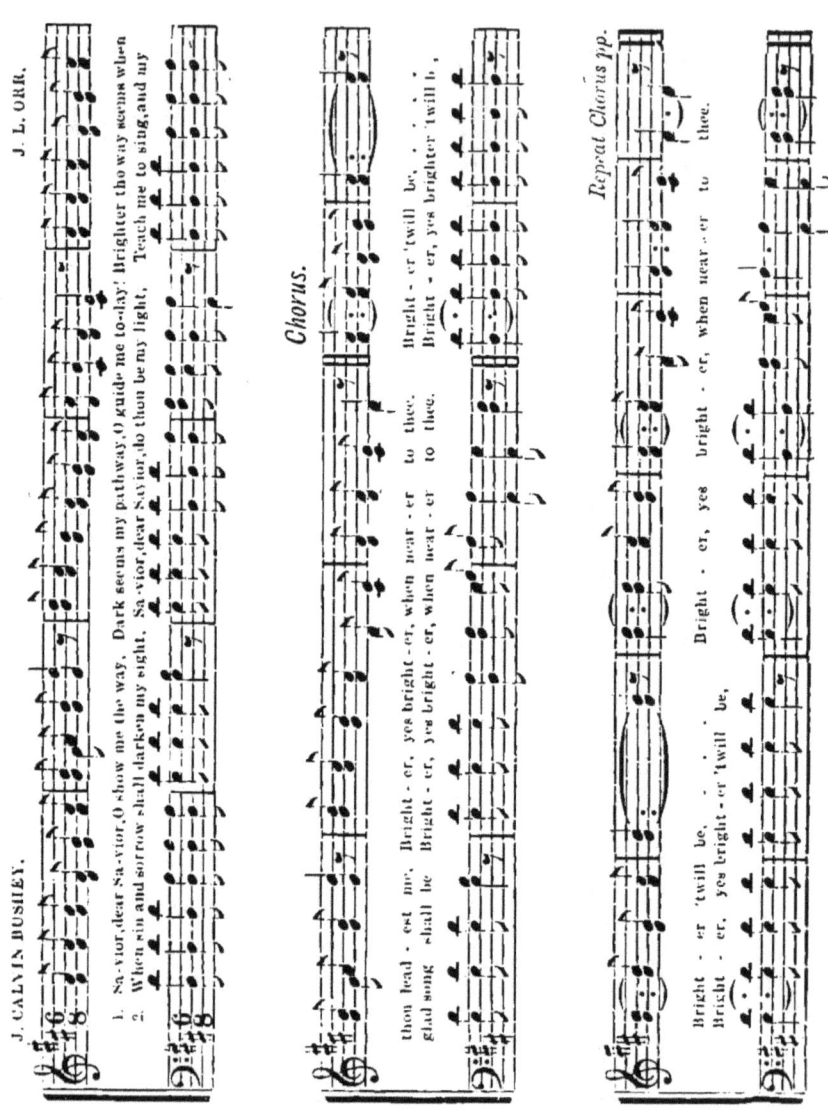

MY HOUSE IS BUILDED ON A ROCK.

Words and Music by J. CALVIN BUSHEY.

1. My house is built up-on a rock, On the rock of Je-sus' love; I will not fear the bil-lows
2. Some build their house up-on the sand, And their Sa-vior not o-bey, And soon the bil-lows and the
3. What a glorious pros-pect is in store, If the Sa-vior is our rock; The wind and waves may loudly

shock, It's foun-da-tions will not move. My house is firm, Twill
wind, Will wash their hopes a-way. house is firm house is firm
roar, We need not fear their shock.

stand the bil-lows shock; My house is firm, 'Tis built up-on a rock.
house is firm, house is firm,

JUST OVER THE RIVER.

To Jennie Greer, Greenville, Ohio.

Music by J. CALVIN BUSHEY.

1. Just be - yond the shin - ing riv - er Lie the sun - ny fields of bliss; I can see as through a shad-ow O - ver in that land of bliss.
2. Just be - yond the shin - ing riv - er, O - pens wide the pearl - y gate; Swing-ing on its gold - en hing - es, Just be - side it an - gels wait.
3. Just be - yond the shin - ing riv - er, Dawns the light of end-less day; Soon we'll join the ho - ly num-ber, Earth-born shad-ows flee a - way.

Chorus.

O - - ver there, . . The O - ver there, Just o - ver there, an - - gels wait. . . O - - ver there, . . At the beau-ti - ful gol - den gate. An-gels wait, the an-gels wait, O-ver there, Just o - ver there,

WHO LOVE HIM MOST?

Words and Music by WILBUR A CHRISTY.

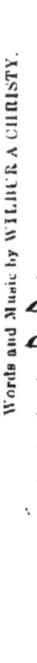

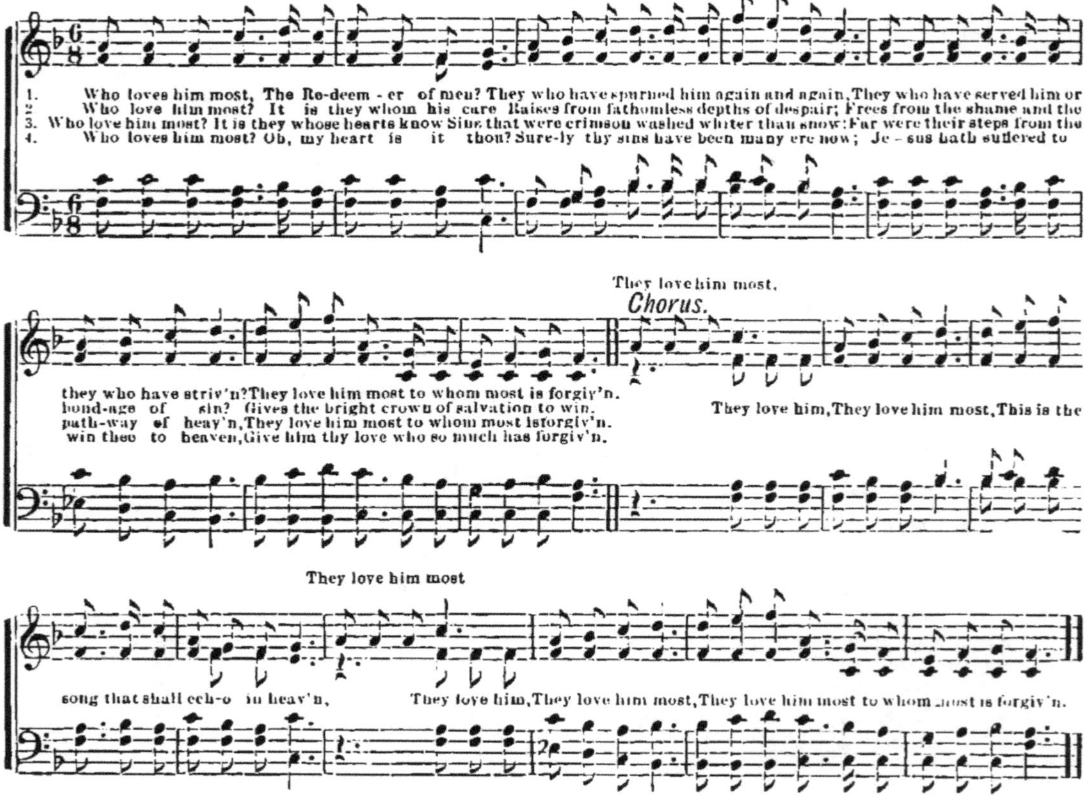

WE SHALL MEET ALL THE LITTLE ONES THERE.

Words and Music by WILL L. THOMPSON.

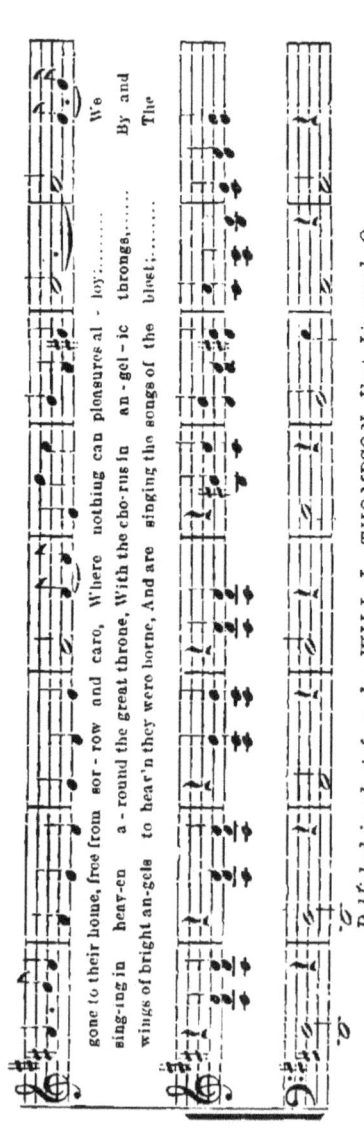

1 Oh where are the lit-tle ones, love-ly and fair, Who once fill'd our hearts full of joy? ...... They have
2 No more shall we see them around the hearth-stone, No more shall we hear their sweet songs; ...... They are
3 Oh why should we sor-row, oh why should we mourn, For the lit-tle ones gone to their rest? ...... On the

gone to their home, free from sor - row and care, Where nothing can pleasures al - loy; .... We
sing-ing in heav-en a - round the great throne, With the cho-rus in an - gel - ic throngs, ... By and
wings of bright an-gels to heav'n they were borne, And are singing the songs of the blest; .... The

Published in sheet form by WILL L. THOMPSON, East Liverpool, O.

WE SHALL MEET ALL THE LITTLE ONES THERE.—Continued.

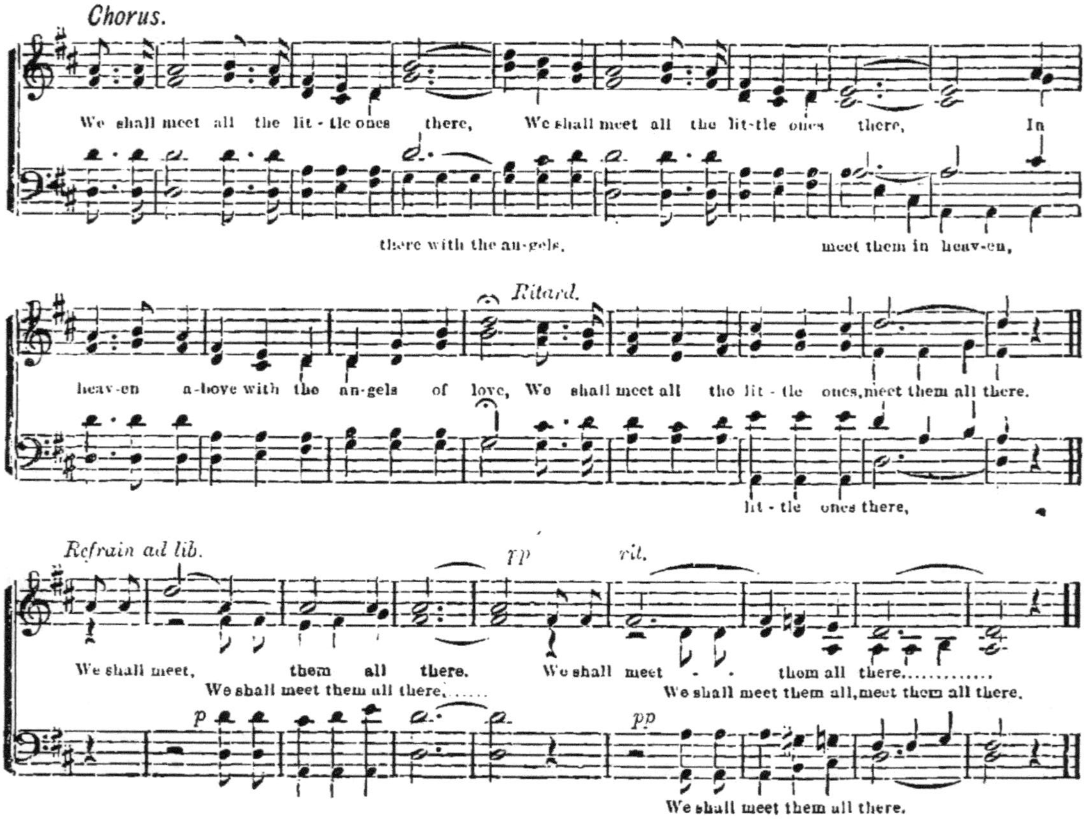
Chorus.
We shall meet all the lit - tle ones there, We shall meet all the lit-tle ones there, In
there with the an-gels, meet them in heav-en,
Ritard.
heav-en a-bove with the an-gels of love, We shall meet all the lit - tle ones, meet them all there.
lit - tle ones there,
Refrain ad lib.
pp
rit.
We shall meet, them all there. We shall meet them all there............
We shall meet them all there,...... We shall meet them all, meet them all there.
p
pp
We shall meet them all there.

LOVING VOICES.

J. CALVIN BUSHEY.

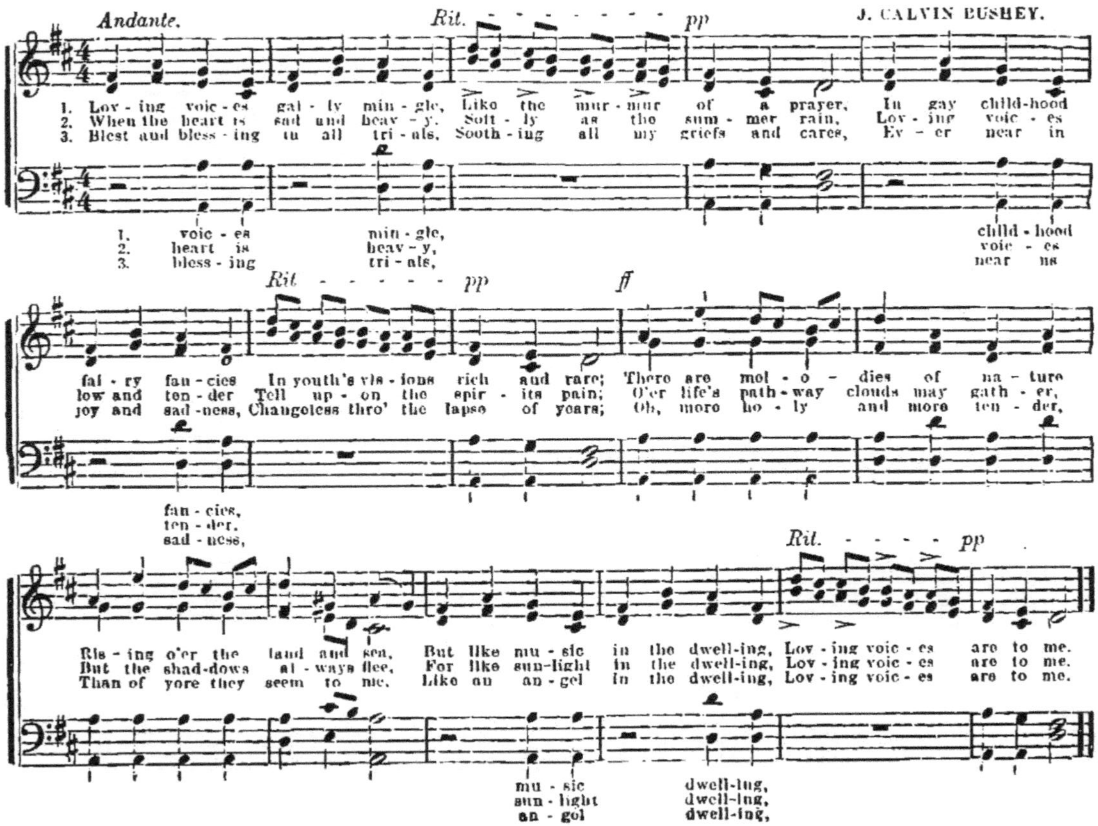

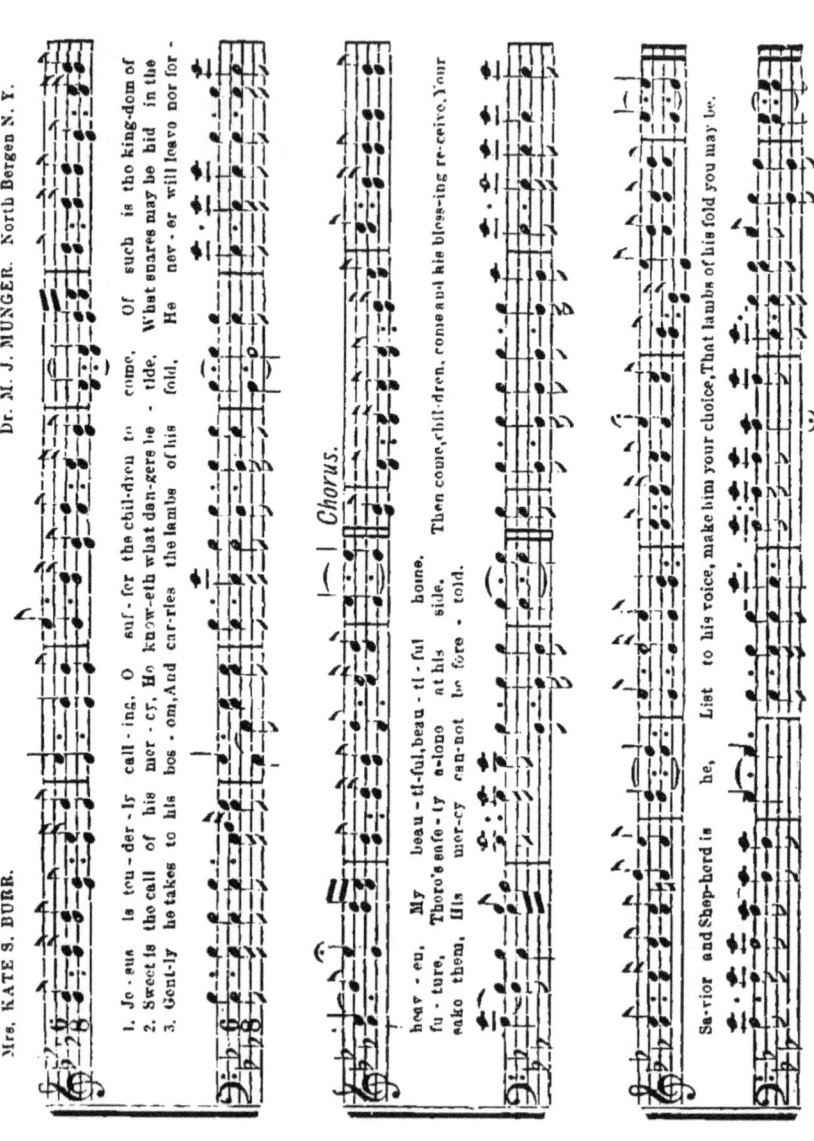

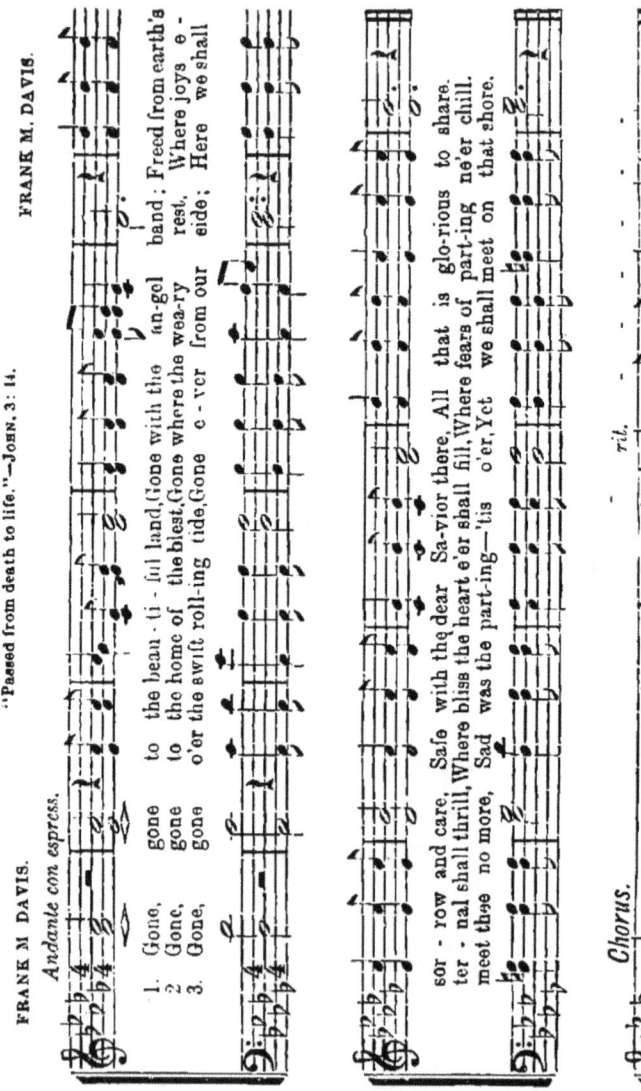

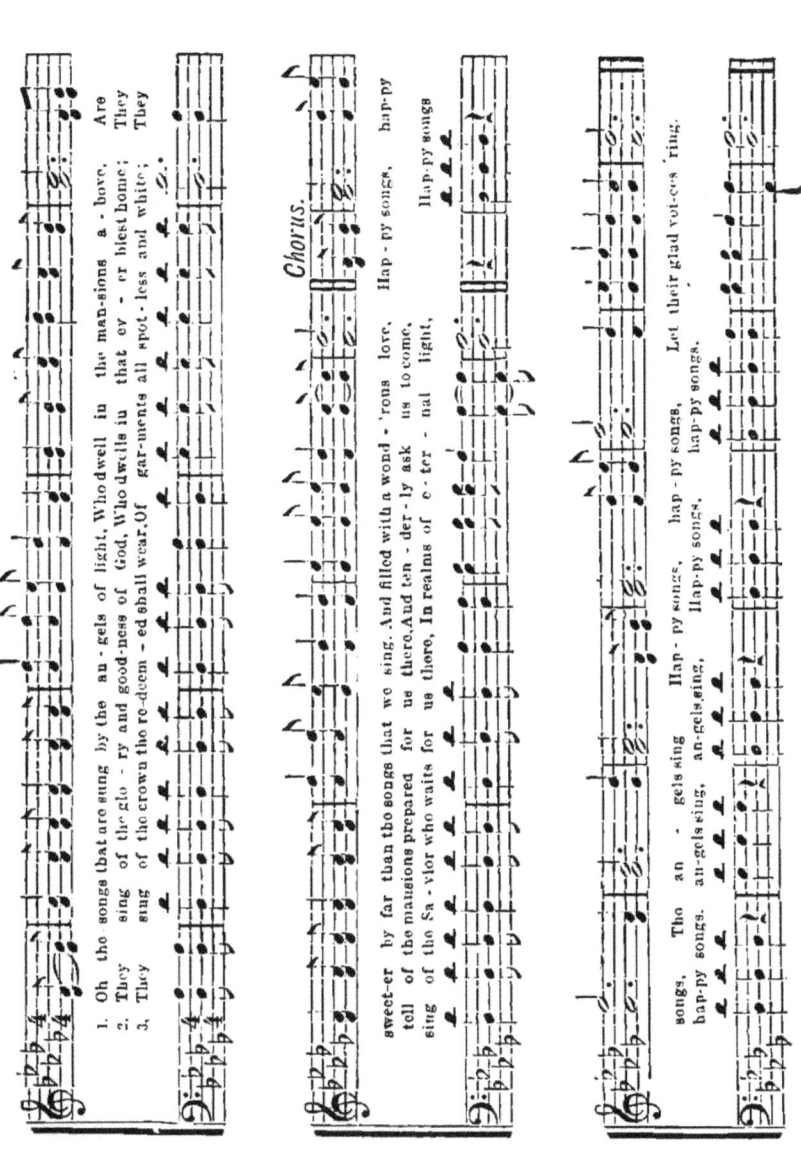

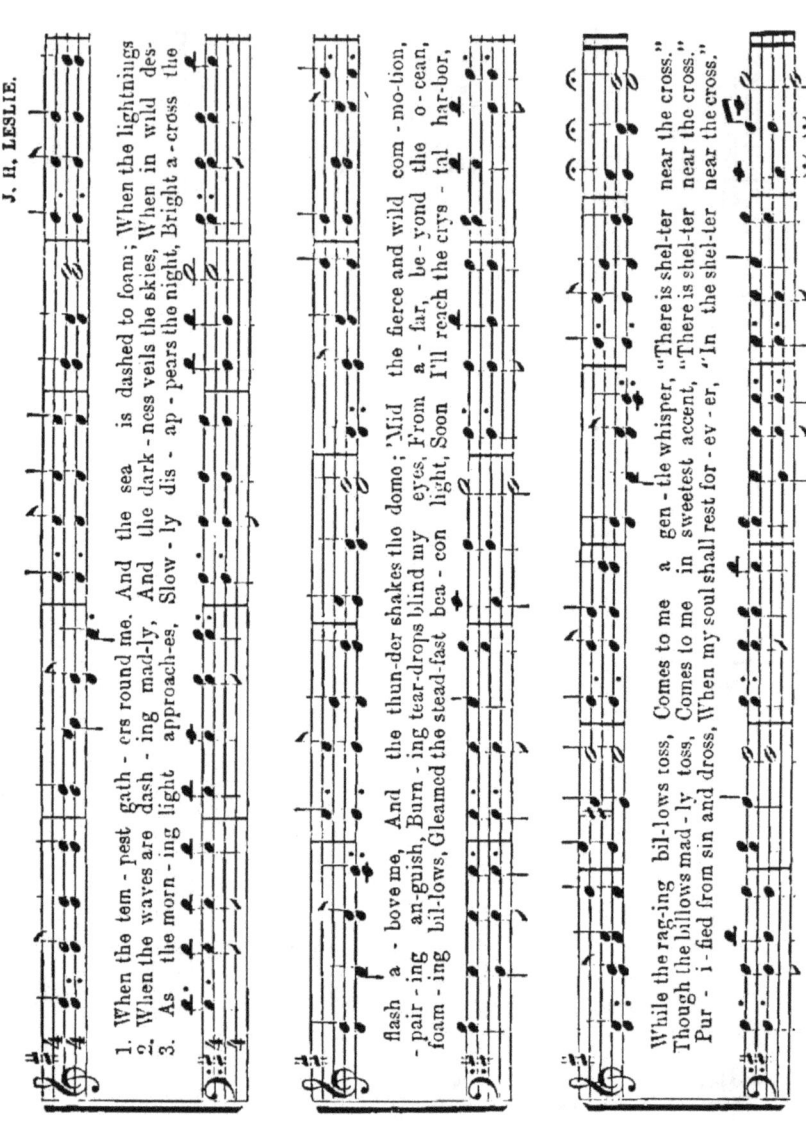

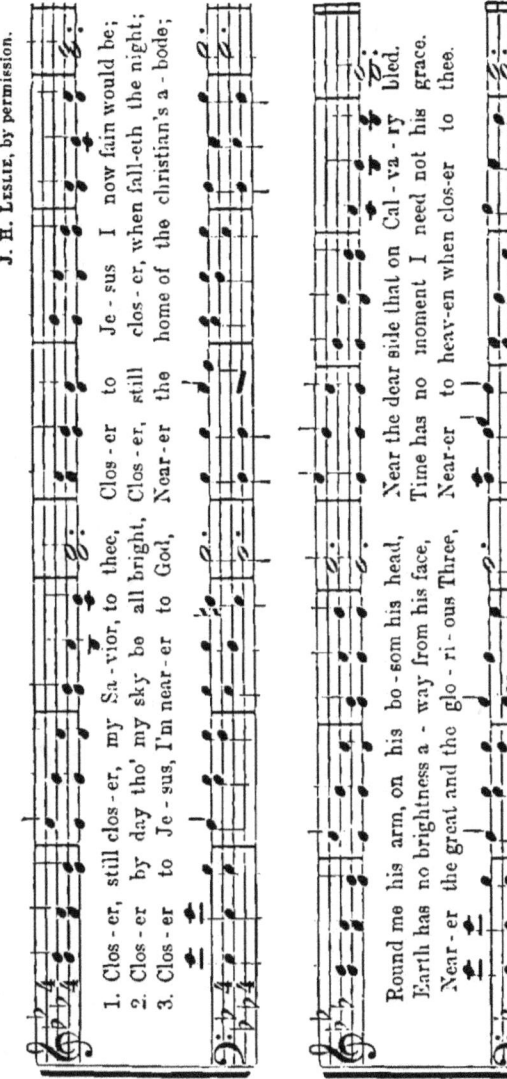
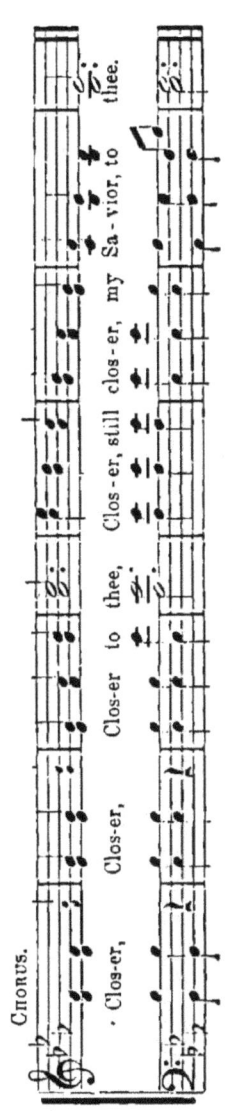

SHOUT THE TIDINGS.

LET YOUR LAMPS BE TRIMMED AND BURNING.

"Watch therefore, for you know neither the day nor the hour wherein the Son of man cometh."—St. Matt. 25. 13.

E. B. LATTA.
FRANZ.

1. As the coming of the Bridegroom, At the midnight's sol-emn hour, So may be our call to judgement, Summoned by Al-migh-ty pow'r!
2. Be not like the fool-ish vir-gins, Who, because the Bridegroom stay'd, Slept and slumber'd all un-heed-ing, And no pre-par-a-tion made, Let your lamps be trimm'd and burning, Trimm'd and
3. Then the wise with oil pro-vid-ed, And their lamps with light aglow, When 'twas said the Bridegroom com-eth, Out to wel-come him did go.
4. Then the fool-ish vir-gins vain-ly, Emp-ty lamps to light did try, And the door was shut a-gainst them, While their oil they went to buy.
5. Let us like the wise be read-y; For the hour we may not know, When the Lord may come to call us, To a place of joy or woe.

Chorus.

burning, Trimm'd and burning, Let your lamps be trimm'd and burning When the Bridegroom shall appear.

Savior, Like A Shepherd.

WILLIAM B. BRADBURY.

1. Sa - vior, like a Shepherd lead us, Much we need Thy tend'rest care;
In Thy pleasant pastures feed us, For Thy folds prepare;
2. We are Thine, do Thou befriend us, Be the guardian of our way;
Keep Thy flock, from sin defend us, Seek us when we go astray;
3. Thou hast promised to receive us, Poor and sinful though we be;
Thou hast mercy to relieve us, Grace to cleanse and pow'r to free;
4. Early let us seek Thy favor, Early let our bosoms all
Blessed Lord and only Savior, With Thy love our bosoms fill.

Bless - ed Je - sus, Bless - ed Je - sus,
Bless - ed Je - sus, Bless - ed Je - sus,
Bless - ed Je - sus, Bless - ed Je - sus,
Bless - ed Je - sus, Bless - ed Je - sus,

Thou hast bought us, Thine we are,
Hear, O hear us, when we pray,
We will early turn to Thee,
Thou hast loved us, love us still.

Just As I Am.

1. Just as I am, without one plea,
But that Thy blood was shed for me,
And that Thou bidd'st me come to Thee,
O Lamb of God! I come, I come!

2. Just as I am and waiting not,
To rid my soul of one dark blot,
To Thee, whose blood can cleanse each spot,
O Lamb of God! I come, I come!

3. Just as I am, though tossed about
With many a conflict, many a doubt,
Fightings and fears within, without,
O Lamb of God! I come, I come!

4. Just as I am, poor, wretched, blind,
Sight, riches, healing of the mind,
Yea, all I need, in Thee to find,
O Lamb of God! I come, I come!

5. Just as I am; Thou wilt receive,
Will welcome, pardon, cleanse, relieve;
Because Thy promise I believe,
O Lamb of God! I come, I come!

We Praise Thee, O God.

1. We praise thee, O God! for the Son of thy love,
For Jesus who died, and is now gone above!
Cho—Hallelujah! thine the glory, Hallelujah! amen,
Hallelujah! thine the glory, revive us again.

2. We praise thee, O God! for thy Spirit of light,
Who has shown us our Savior, and scattered our night.

All glory and praise to the Lamb that was slain,
Who has borne all our sins, and has cleansed every stain.

4. All glory and praise to the God of all grace,
Who has bought us, and sought us, and guided our ways.

What A Friend We Have In Jesus.

1. What a friend we have in Jesus,
All our sins and griefs to bear;
What a privilege to carry
Everything to God in prayer.
Oh, what peace we often forfeit,
Oh, what needless pain we bear—
All because we do not carry
Everything to God in prayer.

2. Have we trials and temptations?
Is there trouble anywhere?
We should never be discouraged,
Take it to the Lord in prayer.
Can we find a Friend so faithful,
Who will all our sorrows share?
Jesus knows our every weakness,
Take it to the Lord in prayer.

3. Are we weak and heavy-laden,
Cumbered with a load o' care?
Precious Savior, still our refuge,
Take it to the Lord in prayer.
Do thy friends despise, forsake thee?
Take it to the Lord in prayer;
In his arms he'll take and shield thee,
Thou wilt find a solace there.

The Lord's Prayer.—Chant.

1. Our Father which art in heaven,...... hallowed be thy name;
2. Give us this day our daily bread; And forgive us our trespasses as we forgive them that trespass against us.
3. And lead us not into temptation, but deliver us from evil: For thine is the kingdom, and the power, and the glory, for-ev-er, A-men.

44. Brighter Day.

EVA CARY.   J. CALVIN BUSHEY.

1. I am waiting, I am watching for the messenger to come, That unbinds my soul from prison, Wafts it to a brighter home, And the
2. I am waiting, I am watching for the lov'd ones on the strand That with bounding steps will meet me In a joyous choral band, Strip me
3. I am waiting, I am watching for the swell of golden light That announces to my vision, The blest haven is in sight, For the
4. I am waiting, I am watching for the blessed voice to hear Bidding me lay down my armor, Trusting in him without fear, He will

tired and weary bod - y Will be laid a-way to rest Where the wicked cease from troubling, In that land among the blest.
of my earthly mantle, Lead me thro' the o-pen door, And with smiles of brightest welcome We will dwell there evermore.
rip-ple of the mu-sic Floating from the oth-er side, Cheering up the weary pilgrim In the bat-tle with the tide.
lead me by the rivers, Wipe my many tears a-way, And his smile will light the shadows To a nev-er-fad-ing day.

CHORUS.

I am wait - ing,   I am watch - ing   For the bright and   hap-py day,

I am waiting, I am watching, I am watching For the bright and happy day, For the bright and happy day, I am

Brighter Day.—Concluded.

walt - - - - ing, I am watch - - - ing.

walt-ing, I am watching, I am waiting, Till the clouds shall pass a-way.   *Repeat Cho. pp*

Trusting In The Lord.

(Closing piece.)

J. CALVIN BUSHEY.

Largo.

Trust in the Lord and do good, Trust in the Lord and do good, So shalt thou dwell in the land, And ver - i - ly,

cres. . . ff   dim

— ver-i-ly, Thou shalt be fed, And ver-i-ly, ver-i-ly, ver-i-ly Thou shalt be fed.

f . . . . p . . . . f . . . . p . . . . Rit . . . .

45

46

Work In My Vineyard.

HATTIE LEWIS. H. A. LEWIS.

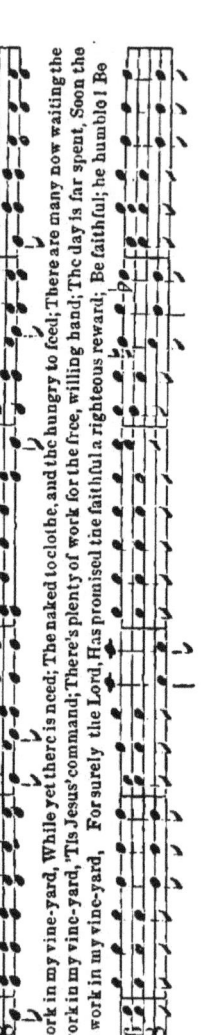

1. Go work in my vine-yard, While yet there is need; The naked to clothe, and the hungry to feed; There are many now waiting the gospel to hear, Oh! tell them of Jesus, Who soon will appear.
2. Go work in my vine-yard, 'Tis Jesus' command; There's plenty of work for the free, willing hand; The day is far spent, Soon the night will come on; Oh! haste while it tarries, That thy work may be done.
3. Go work in my vine-yard, For surely the Lord, Has promised the faithful a righteous reward; Be faithful; he humble! Be earnest and true, And blessing will follow, Your efforts and you.

CHORUS. Work, - - - - go work, - - - -

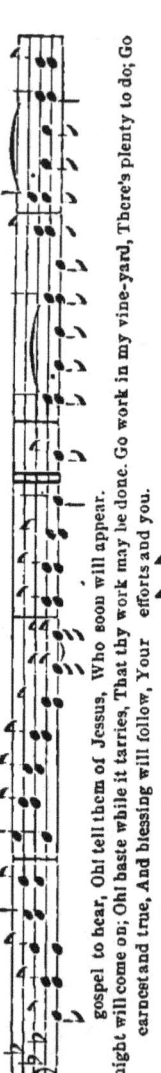

Go work in my vine-yard, There's plenty to do; Go work in my vine-yard, There's plenty to do;

Go - work, - - - - go work, - - - -

work in my vine-yard, While yet it is day, For Jesus, the Master, will surely repay, For Jesus, the master, will surely repay.

Rit. . . . .

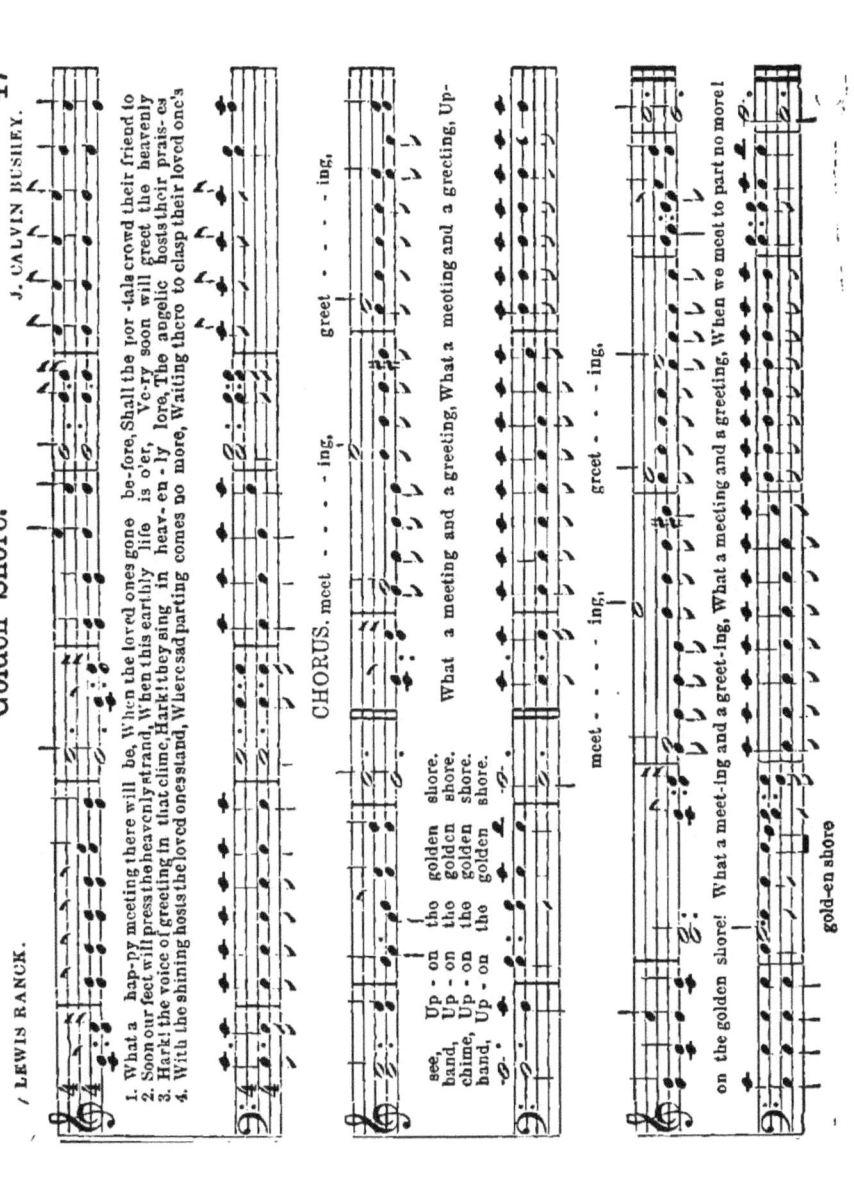

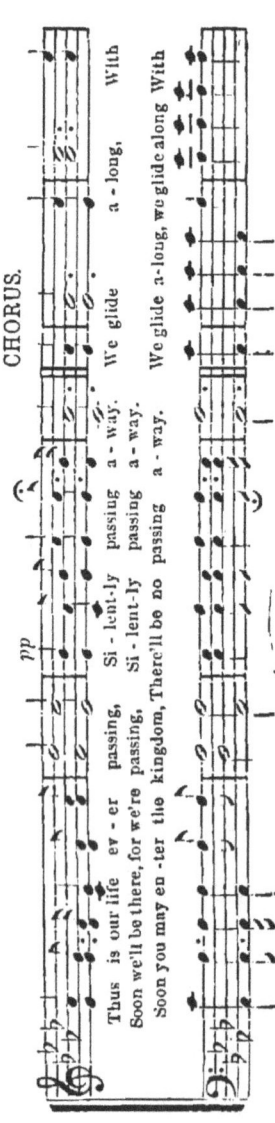

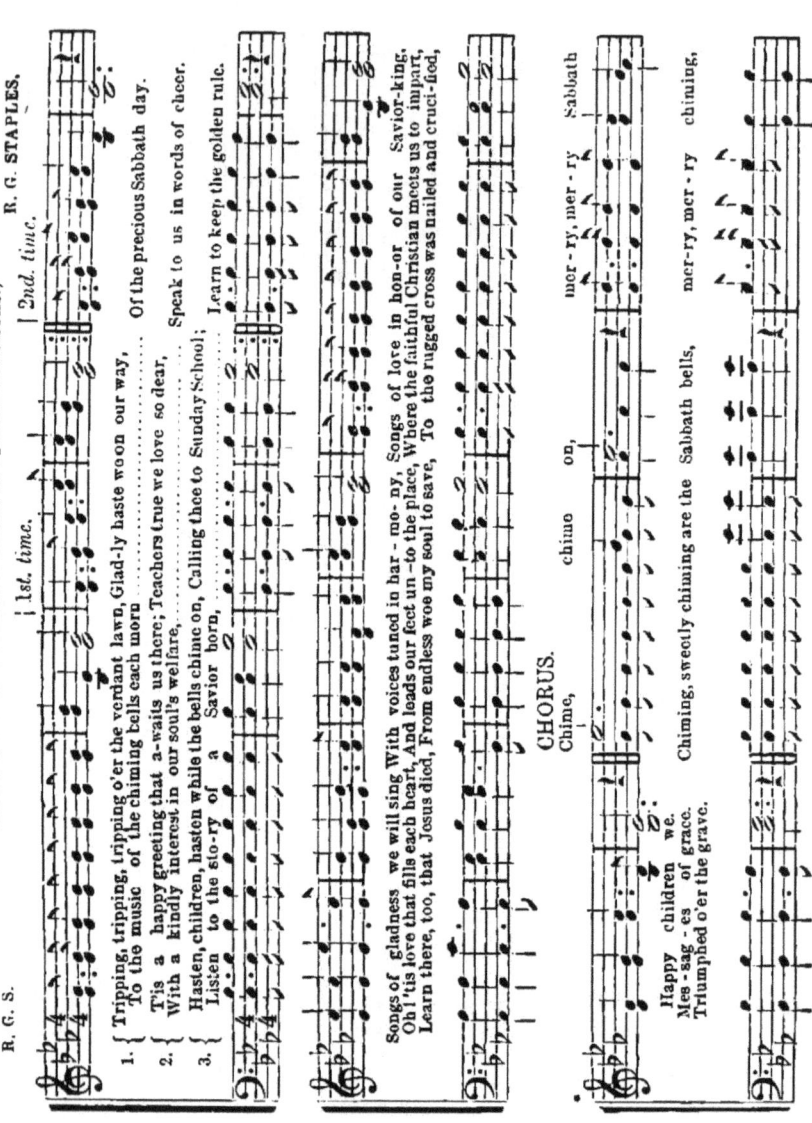

Take Down Your Harps.

Rev. H. R. TUCKETT.
J. H. ROSECRANS.

55

1. By Ba-by-lon's rivers O children of God, No long-er in bondage we weep, Tho
2. Oh! why should we ev-er his prom-is-es doubt, Or fear that his arm can not save, Re-
3. The sun may dissolve and the stars may grow old, The world with its pomp pass a - way, But for-
4. Oh! sing in your gladness, ye saved of the Lord, Dis - miss all your fears, you are free; Your

CHORUS.

God of our fathers, the al-mighty Lord, His ransomed in safety will keep.
deemed from our bondage we joyfully shout, Sal-vation and pardon we have. Then take down your harp from the
ev - er and ev - er thro' a - ges untold, Our God will unchange-a-ble stay.
God who has saved you has pledged you his word, Your God he forever will be.

willows,Strike the chords in the fullness of joy,Sing again the old songs,Sing the God-giv'n songs, Let praise your glad voices employ.

Going Home.

Words and Music by J. CALVIN BUSHEY.

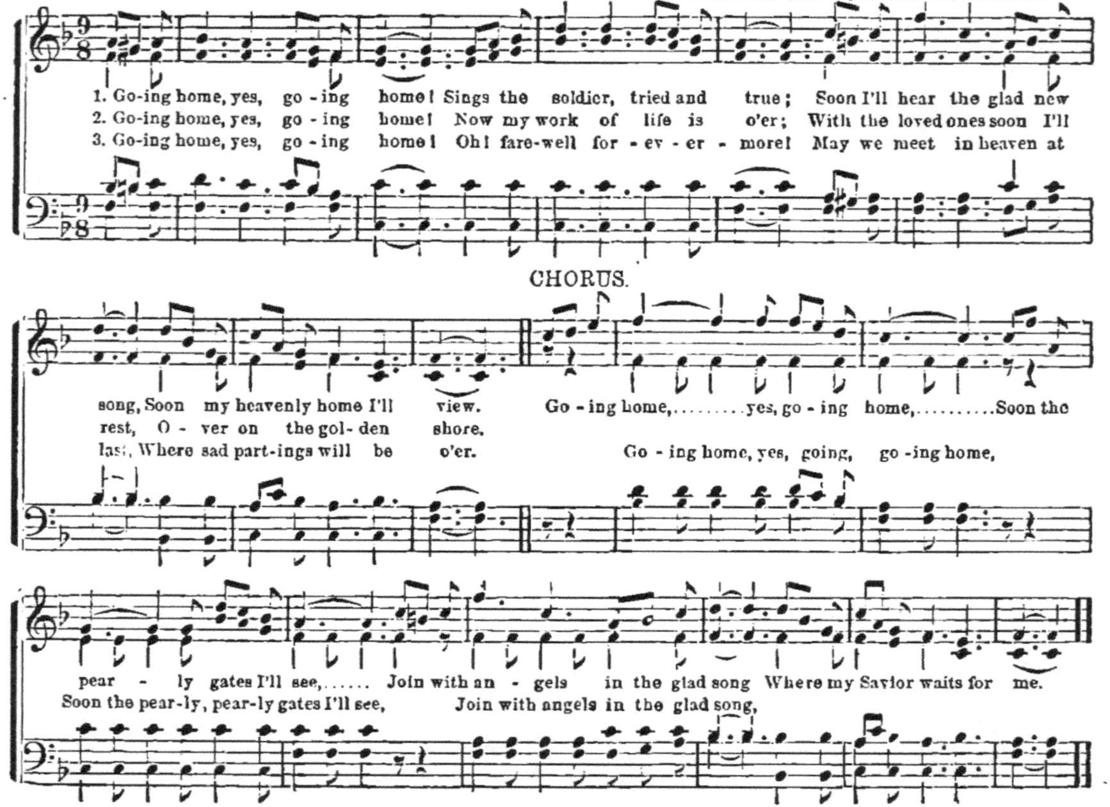

Soldiers Of Christ, Arise. 57

J. CALVIN BUSHEY.

Con spirito.

1. Soldiers of Christ, a - rise, And put your ar - mor on,
2. Stand then against your foes, In close and firm ar - ray,
3. From strength to strength go on, Wrestle and fight and pray,

1. Sol - diers of Christ, a - rise, And put your ar - mor on,
2. Stand then a - gainst your foes, In close and firm ar - ray,
3. From strength to strength go on, Wres - tle and fight and pray,

Strong in the strength which God sup - plies Thro' his e - ter - nal Son.
Le - gion of wil - y fiends op - pose Through-out the e - vil day.
Tread all the powers of dark - ness down, And win the well-fought day.

CHORUS.

A - - rise, a - - rise, And
A - rise, a - rise,

Strong in the strength which God supplies Thro' his e - ter - nal Son.

put your ar - mor on,

Children's Invitation.

Rev. D. R. COLMERY.

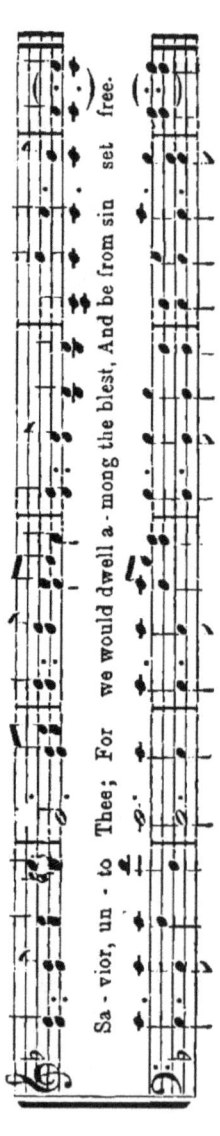

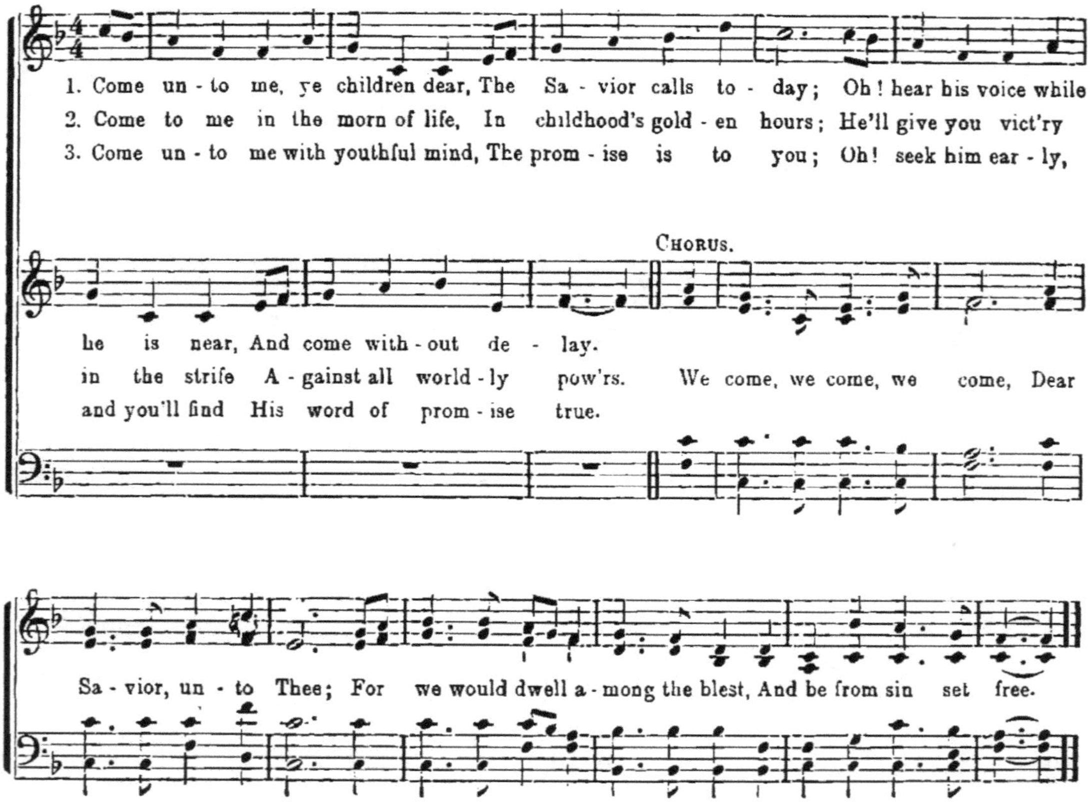

My Beautiful Home.

RAY. L. STOUGHTON. J. CALVIN BUSHEY.

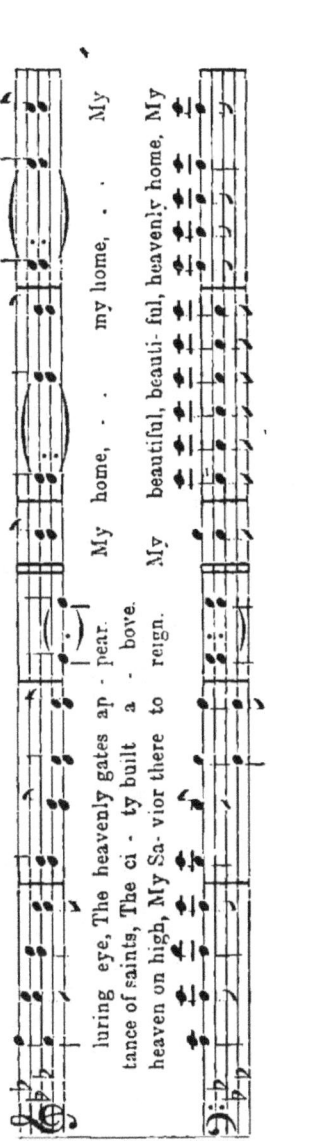

1. O heavenly home on high, Home of my soul, how near! At times to faith's alluring eye, The heavenly gates appear.
2. Ah! then my spirit pants, To reach that land of love, That bright inheritance of saints, The city built above.
3. Oh! then I will not sigh, Nor of my lot complain; For Jesus rose to heaven on high, My Savior there to reign.

CHORUS.

My home, my home, My beautiful, beautiful, heavenly home, My

Beautiful Land Of Rest.—Concluded.

I Long To Be There.

LAMARTINE.

1. My heav'nly home is bright and fair, I long to be there, No pain nor death can enter there, I long to be there.
2. Its glittering tow'rs the sun out-shine, I long to be there, That heav'nly mansion shall be mine, I long to be there.
3. My Father's house is built on high, I long to be there, Far, far a-bove the star-ry sky, I long to be there.
4. When from this earthly prison free, I long to be there, That heav'enly mansion mine shall be, I long to be there.

CHORUS.

Oh! an - gels, guide me home, An - gels, guide me home, I long to be there.

angels, angels, angels, angels.

Copyright, 1880, by WILL L. THOMPSON & Co

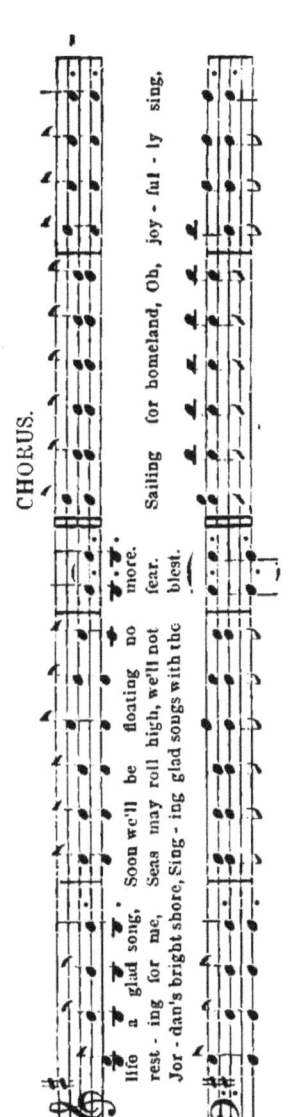

Whiter Than Snow.—Concluded.

Whit - - - - er than snow,......... Lamb......
Whiter than snow, Whiter than the snow, the snow, Wash me in the blood of the lamb, And I shall be whiter than snow, the snow.

Little Lights. (Child's Song.)

J. CALVIN BUSHEY.

1. Je-sus bids us shine, With a pure, clear light, Like a lit-tle can-dle Burning in the night.
2. Je-sus bids us shine, First of all for him, Well he sees and knows it If our light is dim;
3. Je-sus bids us shine, Then, for all a-round, Ma-ny kinds of dark-ness In the world are found;

In this world of darkness, So we must shine, You in your small cor-ner, And I in mine.
He looks down from heav-en, To see us shine, You in your small cor-ner, And I in mine.
Sin, and want, and sor-row, So we must shine, You in your small cor-ner, And I in mine.

Jesus At The Well.

A. S. K.

To HARMAN H. MINGLIN, HUBBARD, OHIO.

J. CALVIN BUSHEY.

1. Je-sus sat by the well, as a woman came there, She a poor needy sinner like me; And He gave her to drink of the wa-ter of life; Now this wa-ter is flowing for thee.
2. Who-so drinketh this water shall thirst nev-er-more; For a fountain it ev-er-shall be, Spring-ing up in thy soul un-to life ev-er-more; Now this wa-ter is flowing for thee.
3. That same well is still full and the Savior still waits; Hear him call, thirsty sinner, for thee; Will you drink of the fountain of life and live, While this wa-ter is flowing for thee?

CHORUS.

Oh! come, then, to the wa - - - ters, Flowing so free,..... Come, then, to the wa - - - ters, Flowing for you and me. Oh! come, then, come unto the waters, Flowing, flowing so free, Come, then, come unto the water.

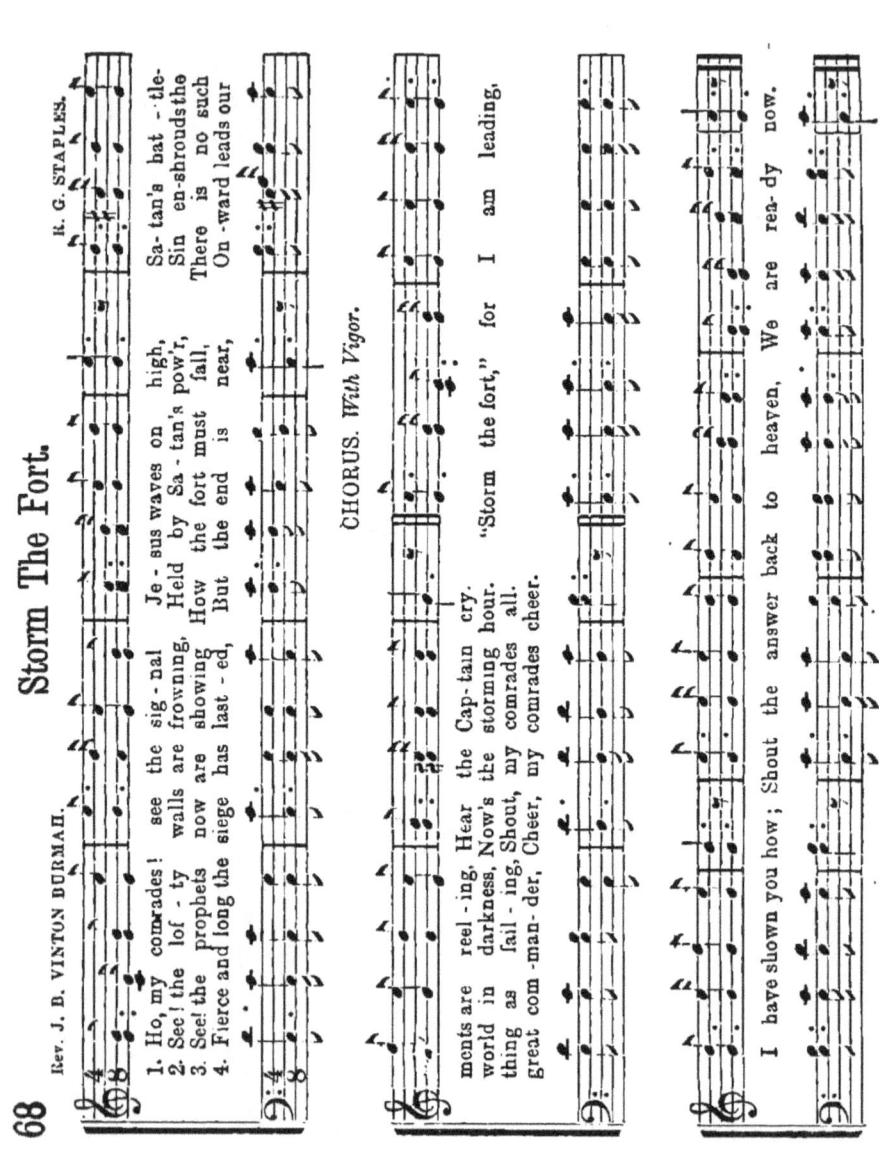

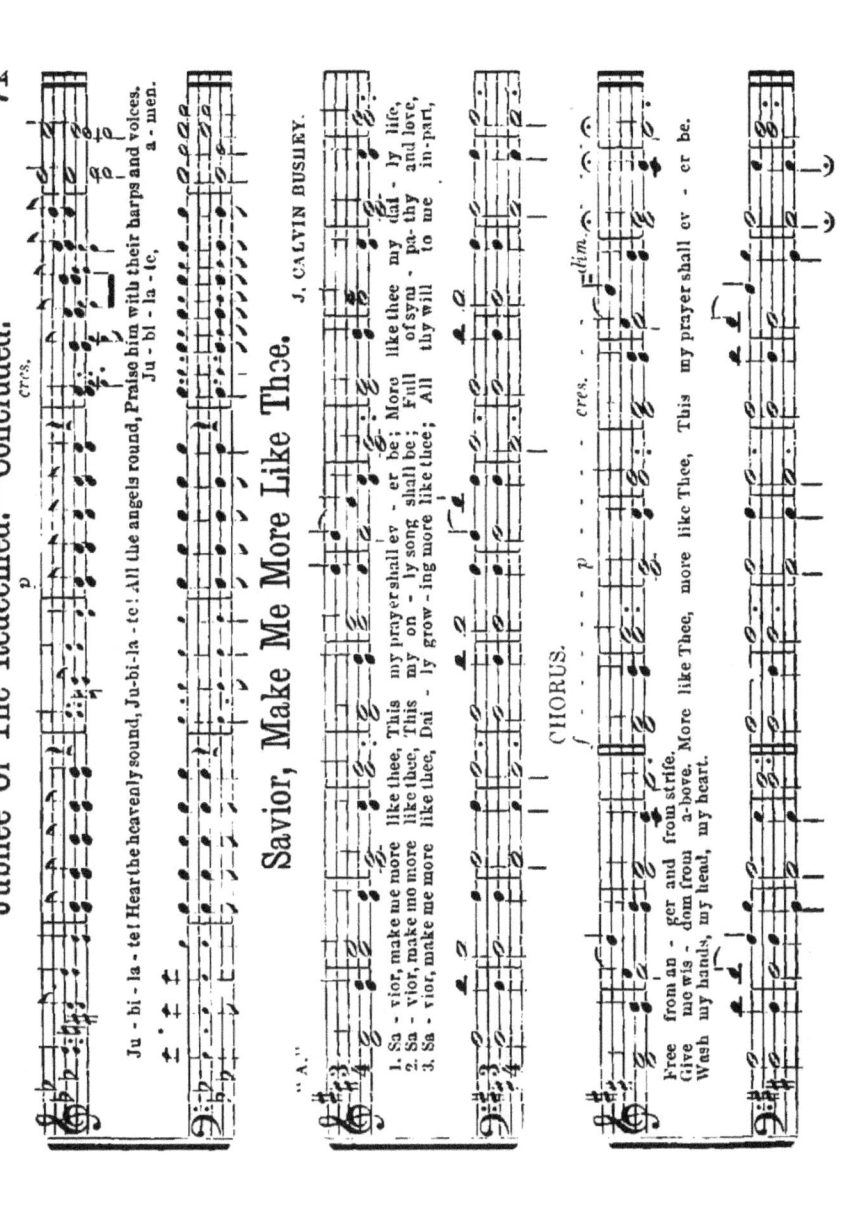

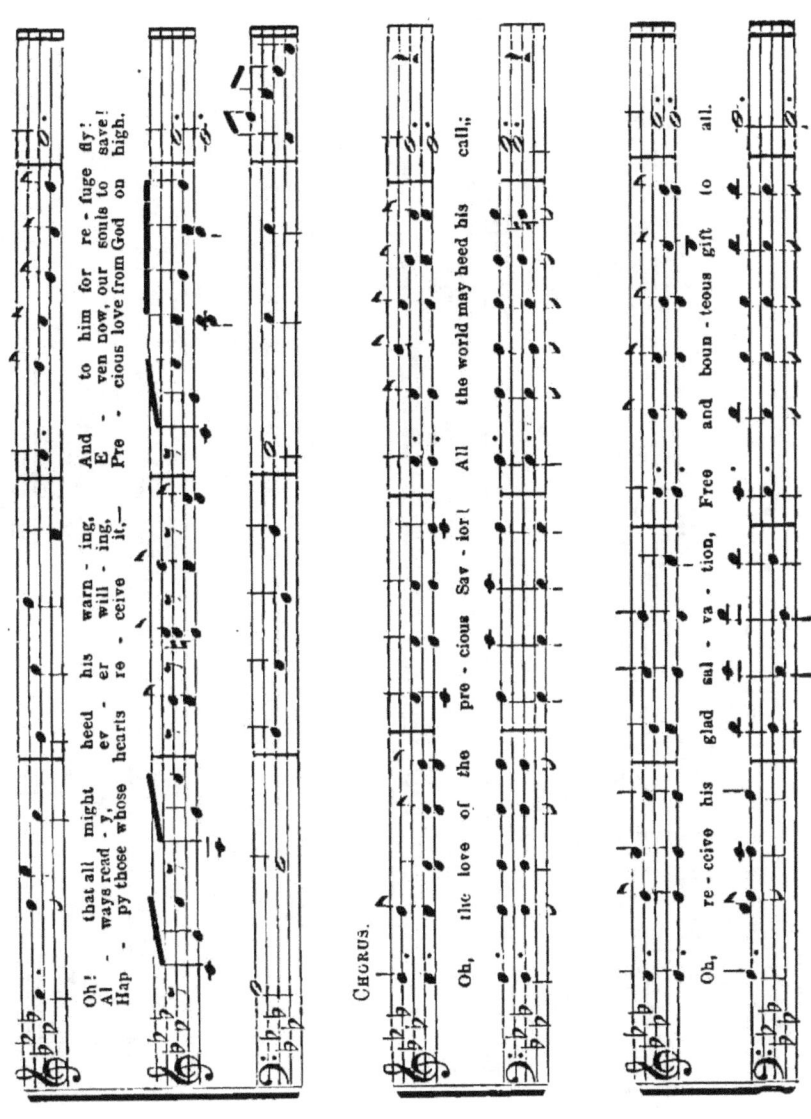

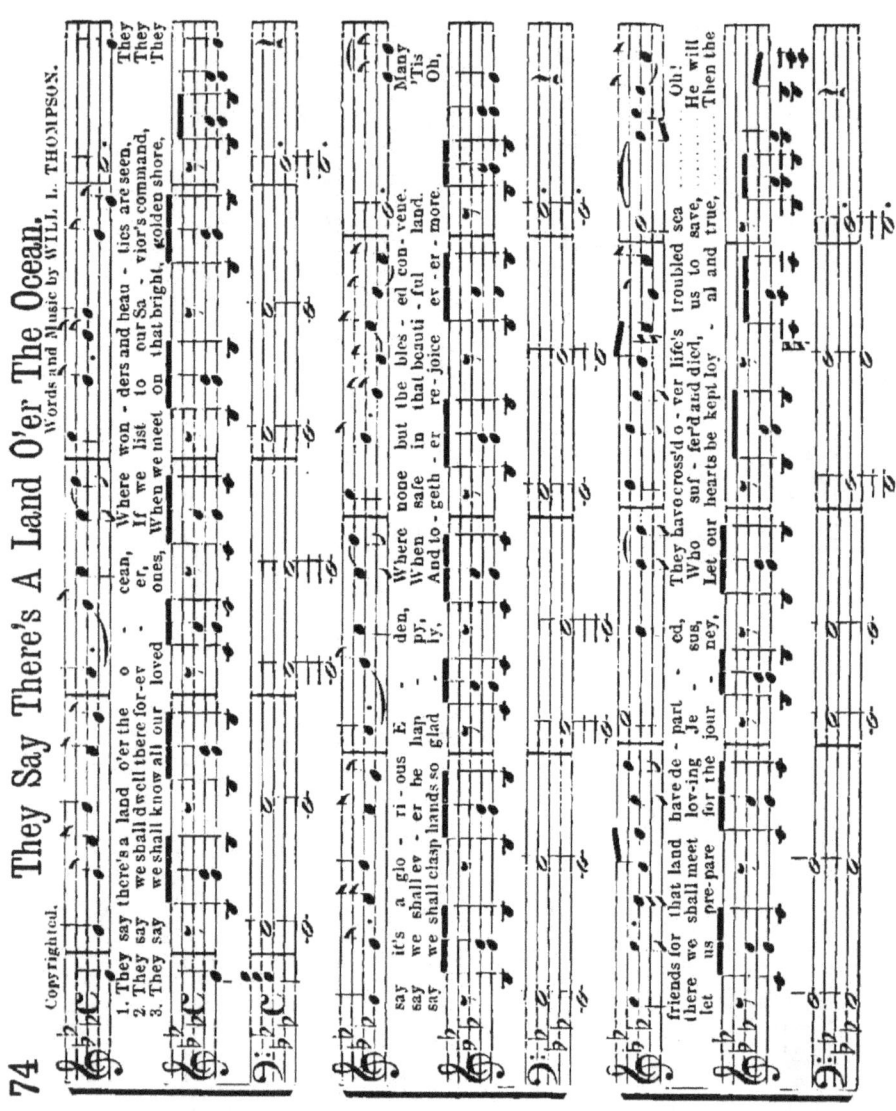

Look To The Comforter.—Concluded.

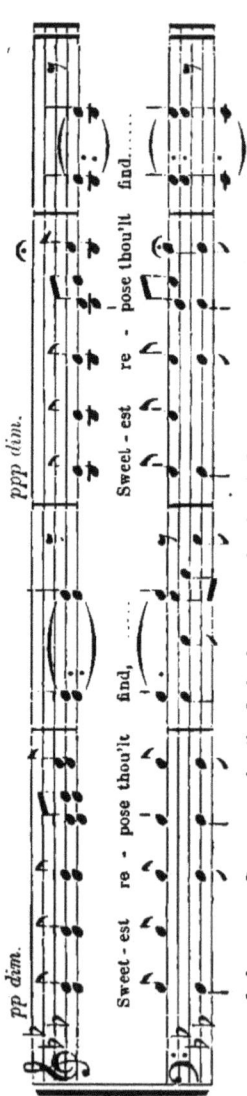

Nearer, My God, To Thee.

1 Nearer, my God, to Thee!
  Nearer to Thee!
  Ev'n though it be a cross
    That raiseth me;
  Still all my song shall be—
  Nearer, my God, to Thee,
    Nearer to Thee!

2 Though, like the wanderer,
    The sun gone down,
  Darkness be over me,
    My rest a stone;
  Yet in my dreams I'd be
  Nearer, my God, to Thee—
    Nearer to Thee!

3 There let the way appear,
    Steps unto heaven;
  All that Thou sendest me,
    In mercy given;
  Angels to beckon me
  Nearer, my God, to Thee—
    Nearer to Thee!

4 Then with my waking thoughts,
    Bright with Thy praise,
  Out of my stony griefs,
    Bethel I'll raise;
  So by my woes to be
  Nearer, my God to Thee!
    Nearer to Thee!

My Faith Looks Up To Thee.

1 My faith looks up to Thee,
    Thou Lamb of Calvary,
        Savior divine!
  Now hear me while I pray,
  Take all my sins away,
  Oh, let me from this day
        Be wholly Thine.

2 May Thy rich grace impart
  Strength to my fainting heart;
        My zeal inspire:
  As Thou hast died for me,
  O may my love to Thee,
  Pure, warm, and changeless be,
        A living fire.

3 While life's dark maze I tread,
  And griefs around me spread,
        Be Thou my guide:
  Bid darkness turn to day,
  Wipe sorrow's tears away,
  Nor let me ever stray,
        From Thee aside

4 When ends life's transient dream,
  When death's cold, sullen stream
        Shall o'er me roll,
  Blest Savior, then in love,
  Fear and distrust remove,
  O bear me safe above,
        A ransomed soul!

Work, For The Night Is Coming.

1 Work, for the night is coming,
  Work through the morning hours;
  Work, while the dew is sparkling,
    Work, 'mid springing flowers;
  Work when the day grows brighter,
    Work in the glowing sun;
  Work, for the night is coming,
    When man's work is done.

2 Work, for the night is coming;
    Work through the sunny noon
  Fill brightest hours with labor,
    Rest comes sure and soon ;
  Give every flying minute
    Something to keep in store;
  Work, for the night is coming
    When man works no more.

3 Work, for the night is coming,
    Under the sunset skies,
  While their bright tints are glowing,
    Work, for daylight flies;
  Work till the last beam fadeth,
    Fadeth to shine no more;
  Work, while the night is darkening,
    When man's work is o'er.

The Promised Land.

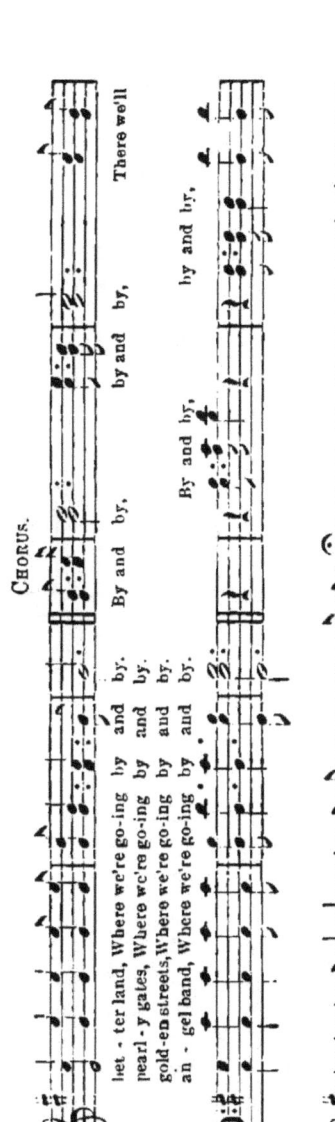

Angels Ring On!	5
Beautiful Land of Rest	60
Beautiful Vale of Rest	18
Brighter Day	44
Brighter When Nearer to Thee	6
Children's Invitation	58
Christus Victor	19
City of God	32
Clinging to the Cross	24
Closer to Thee	37
Even Me	23
Forbid Them Not	30
For You and for Me	54
Going Home	56
Golden Shore	47
Gone to the Beautiful Land	34
Happy Songs	35
Hosanna to our King	11
I Long to be There	61
In the Shelter of the Rock	4
Is My Name Written There?	69
Jerusalem, my Happy Home	66
Jesus, at the Well	67
Jesus Calls Thee	53
Jesus Will be There	17
Just Beside the River	15
Just Over the River	9
Jubilee of the Redeemed	70
Lead Me Gently Home, Father	26
Let Your Lamps be Trimmed and Burning	30
Little Children Should Love Jesus	3
Little Lights	65
Look to the Comforter	76
Loving Voices	29
Mighty to Save	13
My Beautiful Home	59

My Faith Looks up to Thee	78
My House is Built upon a Rock	7
My Mother's Grave	51
My Work is nearly Done	48
Nearer, My God, to Thee	78
No Night in Heaven	10
Nothing, Lord, have I to Bring	49
One by One	40
Sabbath Chimes	52
Sailing for Homeland	63
Saviour, like a Shepherd	41
Saviour, make me more like Thee	71
Shelter Near the Cross	36
Shout the Tidings	38
Silently Passing Away	50
Singing Glory, Hallelujah	25
Singing with the Angels	14
Soldiers of Christ, Arise!	57
Storm the Fort	68

Take down your Harps	55
The Lord's Prayer	42
There's a Land o'er the Ocean	74
There is a Clime, a Cloudless Clime	28
The Promised Land	79
They say there's a Land o'er the Ocean	74
'Tis sweet to know that Jesus loves us	72
To Thee, O Lord	62
Trusting in the Lord	45
Walk in the Light	8
We all have a Work to do	33
We are going Home	43
We shall meet all the Little Ones there	20
We'll meet to part no more	31
What a Friend we have in Jesus	42
Whiter than Snow	64
Who love Him most	12
Work, for the Night is coming	78
Work in my Vineyard	46

NOTE.—Pages 3, 34 and 39 are taken from "Always Welcome," by the kind permission of the Publisher.

www.ingramcontent.com/pod-product-compliance
Lightning Source LLC
Chambersburg PA
CBHW031606110426
42742CB00037B/1303